CAREERS INSIDE THE WORLD OF

Entrepreneurs

An endless number of business opportunities are open to a potential
entrepreneur.

CAREERS & OPPORTUNITIES

CAREERS INSIDE THE WORLD OF
Entrepreneurs

by Sue Hurwitz

GLOBE FEARON EDUCATIONAL PUBLISHER
A Division of Simon & Schuster
Upper Saddle River, New Jersey

Published in 1995 by The Rosen Publishing Group, Inc.
29 East 21st Street, New York, NY 10010

First Edition
Copyright © 1995 by The Rosen Publishing Group, Inc.

Library of Congress Cataloging-in-Publication Data

Hurwitz, Sue, 1934–
        Careers inside the world of entrepreneurs / by Sue Hurwitz.—1st
    ed.
            p.   cm. — (Careers & opportunities)
        Includes bibliographical references and index.
        ISBN 0-835-91347-3
        1. Vocational guidance—Juvenile literature. 2. Entrepreneurship—
    Juvenile literature. [1. Entrepreneurship. 2. Businessmen. 3.
    Occupations] I. Title. II. Series
    HF5381.2.H87   1995
    331.7'02—dc20   95-16192
                                                                          CIP
                                                                          AC
Manufactured in the United States of America.

Contents

INTRODUCTION

Who are entrepreneurs? What do they do?

Entrepreneurs are people who organize and run their own business. Usually, they are risk-takers. They are self-starters. They are confident, and they enjoy a challenge. They are not afraid of hard work or long hours. They are patient. They realize that most new businesses take many years before they earn a profit.

We have all heard about successful entrepreneurs. George Parker invented his first board game at age 16. In 1883, George and his brothers formed George S. Parker Company. Their company still manufactures many games, including Monopoly.

W.K. Kellogg developed cornflakes in 1896. Today the Kellogg Company is a major manufacturer of breakfast cereals—including cornflakes.

In 1903, Henry Ford developed the first Model T car while tinkering in his garage. Today, Ford Motors is a huge company.

In 1948, Maurice (Mac) and Richard

The late Henry Ford is shown at the wheel of the Model A Ford Runabout.

McDonald opened a new type of restaurant, which prepared only a few items of food but served them quickly. This fast-food restaurant idea became an immediate success. In 1955, Ray Kroc bought franchise rights from the McDonalds. Ray Kroc later bought the company. Today, he has franchised over 10,000 McDonald's restaurants.

A franchise is an agreement between one company and another. The head company gives an

McDonald's, made famous by Ray Kroc, is one of the world's most popular and well-known franchises.

independently owned company the right to use its name, product, trademark, and operating methods. It often helps the new company owners start up and operate their business. In return, the new company agrees to pay the head company some of its profits.

Not all entrepreneurs get rich from their ideas and hard work. Superman was written and drawn by two seventeen-year-old high school students from Cleveland. In 1934, Jerry Siegel wrote the comic strip and Joe Shuster drew the characters. Superman is big business today, but Siegel and Shuster received little money from it, nor did they become famous.

Sometimes a hobby can lead to a business opportunity like free-lance photography.

Why do people become entrepreneurs if not all entrepreneurs become rich or famous? There are probably as many reasons as there are entrepreneurs!

Some people become entrepreneurs to solve a problem. In 1928, Dan Gerber started manufacturing baby food because his wife was spending all day mashing vegetables for their baby. Today, Gerber Products makes more than 187 varieties of baby food.

Some people become famous entrepreneurs by luck or by accident. William Wrigley, Jr. sold baking powder. In 1892, he began manufacturing

9

Steve Jobs, former Chairman of the Board of Apple Computers, created the user-friendly Macintosh.

chewing gum as a bonus for customers who bought his baking powder. Wrigley's gum, not the baking powder, made him rich and famous.

Some people become entrepreneurs because they crave the challenge of trying something different. Some like the excitement and freedom of working on their own. Some have an idea or a product that they feel they "must" try out.

This book looks at careers in the world of entrepreneurs. It tells how to find career opportunities. It helps you make a business plan. It shows how some people became entrepreneurs.

Building a career is no simple matter. But it is done by many people every day. With a little bit of luck and a lot of hard work, you may become an entrepreneur. You may even become rich or famous!

You must rely on your skills and knowledge to help you choose a career.

CHAPTER 1

A CAREER AS AN ENTREPRENEUR

Today, the North American economy is shaped by global events and international business. No one knows which careers will be best in the future. No one can say that a field will be "it" for even the next ten years.

The average young person today has six or seven different jobs, or minicareers, during his or her working lifetime. Your first career probably will not be your last. Over time, your interests and experience will change. The workplace will change.

So how do you find a business from among the thousands of available careers? The best place to start is by building on your previous choices. Your attitude, your schoolwork, your jobs, and your hobbies are all part of past choices. What you are doing now is part of your decision process.

13

Think about your interests and skills. Think about the things you like to do. Think about the things you hate to do. Think about your experience and education. Think about things you do well.

Read over the following Interests and Skills Inventory and jot down your answers. Your notes can act as a guide to help you plan a career.

Interests and Skills Inventory

1. Are you able to take responsibility?
2. Are you willing to stay with a business during rough times?
3. Is there something that you do well? Do you have a hobby that other people can use?
4. In what subjects do you make your best grades?
5. Do you have experience from volunteer work or a job in some field?
6. Do you plan ahead? Do you have willpower and self-discipline? Do you manage your time well?
7. Will you need more training or education to prepare you for the career? Are you willing to obtain that?
8. Are you outgoing? Do you enjoy the company of other people? Do you like talking with adults? Do you enjoy talking with children?
9. Do you like to work alone?

A part-time job can often help you learn the skills necessary to be a successful entrepreneur.

10. Do you enjoy working with computers? Are you mechanically inclined?
11. Would you rather work indoors or outdoors?
12. Do you have an idea for a good and different product or service?
13. Can you get money to make enough products to start a business?
14. Do you understand that owning your own business often means working long hours?
15. What are your talents? Are you a musician or an artist? Are you organized? Can you keep good records?

One thing to consider when choosing a career is whether you want to work inside or outside.

16. Do you understand that you may lose your savings if your business fails?
17. Can you adapt to changing conditions?

Look over your answers to the Interests and Skills Inventory. Are you still interested in becoming an entrepreneur? Do you have a better

Take advantage of your resources at school to explore possible entrepreneurial options.

idea of what kind of entrepreneur you might like to become?

For example, if your answer to #8 shows that you enjoy children, you might consider the field of child care. If your answer to #8 shows that you prefer adults, you might explore sales. If #9 shows that you prefer to work alone, you might consider fields with little personal contact.

Compare your inventory answers to the following list of Sample Careers. Do you see a match between your talents and a specific area?

Sample Entrepreneur Careers

Arts—manufacturer of art products, entertainer, disc jockey, illustrator, jewelry designer, party planner, photographer of people or pets, musician, singer, calligrapher, or signmaker

Business—worker in advertising, marketing, public relations, mailing, reproduction and steno services, telephone wake-up or message service

Home Repair Services—air conditioning/heating or electrical repair, carpentry, chimney repair, furniture making/repair, garden/lawn services, home appliance/power tool repair, painting, plumbing, roofing, wallpapering

Food Service—caterer, servers for parties, party planner, food specialty maker for catering services

Information/Service Technology—word pro-

The trend of business is moving toward service-based jobs, such as messenger services.

cessor, computer technician, desktop publishing, writer, temporary employment agency

Outdoor Careers—farmer selling produce to restaurants, fish farmer, flower growing and sales, wildlife photographer/artist, free-lance writer, window washer, lawn services

Personal Services—barber/hairstylist, child sitter, dance/physical exercise instructor, tutor/teacher, dressmaker/tailor, housekeeper, housesitter, security patrol service, shopping service

Retail Sales—sale of sporting goods, toys, bird feeders, hobby items, children's play sets, miniature doll houses, recycled clothing/sports equipment

Choose your products carefully. Be sure there is a market for them.

Seasonal Careers—removing snow, making holiday crafts or decorations, landscape architecture

Transportation—courier, chauffeur, auto repairer, travel agent/guide

As you begin to narrow your options, explore each area. Gather information to help you make a decision. Talk to others in the field about their work. Discuss the area with your parents and school counselor. Check out library books and read about the field.

Do volunteer work to learn more about a field. A part-time job can help you find out if it

A small business can turn into a franchise, as Boston Chicken did.

is really as exciting as it looks. Joining an after-school club or activity can give you experience.

Education is your key to a successful entrepreneurial career, no matter what field you choose. The future will hold fewer jobs for uneducated or unskilled workers. The trend is away from industrial jobs to an information- and service-based economy.

High school students can take technical courses and business courses to help prepare them to become entrepreneurs. After high school graduation, technical schools or colleges can help young adults learn valuable skills. The military also offers education and on-the-job training for those who qualify.

Careers in personal services, day care, and food preparation are expanding. Careers in computer services, education, environmental cleanup, and home maintenance are also fast-growing fields. It is estimated that by 1995 there will be 91.3 million workers in service industries.

Choosing an entrepreneurial career is an important decision. You will learn a lot about yourself in the process. You will learn a lot about the workplace. Then you will be able to choose a career that is right for you.

After you decide on a field, you should do some market research. Are there many similar businesses already in your area? Would the competition be too great to start another business?

Check the sales price of products offered in stores. Could you make a profit on your product by selling slightly below the established price? Make a sample product and ask potential customers if they would buy it.

If your idea still sounds good, you are ready to make a business plan.

Allie

I make and sell wearable art—ceramic earrings and barrettes. I've always enjoyed working with art materials. In school I made my best grades in art classes.

I knew just what I wanted to do after high school graduation. I wanted to become an entrepreneur. But I needed to find a product that I would enjoy creat-

ing. I wanted a product that would not take much time or money to make.

I made a quilt during 10th grade. I worked on it every evening and on weekends for seven months, and I sold it to a neighbor for two hundred dollars. But making quilts took too much time and work, so I decided to explore jewelry.

Last summer I began planning my career. I read arts and crafts magazines from the library. I read jewelry-making magazines. I studied the advertisements in the backs of the magazines to learn about supplies and suppliers. I shopped in several local art supply stores.

I found a clay used to make jewelry. It is similar to the clay that children play with, it is easy to use, and it comes in several colors. The clay hardens to look like plastic after being baked in a regular oven.

I bought two different brands of clay to test them. I also bought metal hardware to make earrings and barrettes.

I let the first batch of earrings bake too long, and they scorched. But soon I learned how to control the quality. Making the jewelry was easy and fun. It was quick and cheap. I made two dozen earrings in four hours. The clay for each pair cost twenty-five cents, the hardware about a dime. So for thirty-five cents I had a custom-made product!

Then I worked on how to market it. I figured that smaller stores were more likely to deal with small

As an entrepreneur, you can teach your skills to others, as this dance instructor teaches young girls ballet in her studio.

suppliers. So I went to about ten small stores and boutiques and priced their products.

I found products similar to mine selling for eight to ten dollars. I decided to price my products allowing a 50 percent mark-up for the store. That meant that I would ask $4.00 to $5.00 for my products. At that price, I would make a profit of about $3.50 to $4.50 for each item I sold. For each batch of product, a batch being two dozen, my profit would average about $95.00!

I found an old briefcase to use as a display case. I cut a piece of cardboard to fit the case, covered it with a piece of velvet, and attached my earrings and barrettes to it.

Once I had my display case ready, I concentrated on the business end of my sales. I chose a name for *my business. I went to an office supply store and bought invoices and receipts.*

I wrote a sample sales talk. I practiced displaying my products to my family and friends as I rehearsed my sales talk. Then I dressed neatly and took my case of products out to sell. The first boutique I tried bought my entire inventory on the spot. And paid cash for it!

Now I had a business. I opened a bank account and deposited my sales money, and I set up a schedule for running my business.

Three days a week I produce inventory. One day a week I buy supplies, do recordkeeping and paperwork, and get the inventory ready for market. Two days a week I call on customers and potential customers.

I have been an entrepreneur for over a year now. I am saving money for expansion, and I hope to open my own boutique by next year. Then I will hire someone to help with sales so I can have more time to make products. I plan to start a new line of ethnic jewelry.

Questions to Ask Yourself

There are many different fields you could explore as an entrepreneur. Everything from art to science and math is open to you in some way. Think about what area you would want to specialize in. 1) What interests or skills do you need to become a successful entrepreneur? 2) What kind of business would you like to be involved in? 3) Why do you want to be an entrepreneur?

You may already possess the skills necessary to begin your own business.

CHAPTER 2

BUSINESS BASICS FOR ENTREPRENEURS

Planning is the most important part of running a successful business. Marketing is the most important part of planning. What potential sales do you hope to achieve in three years? How big do you hope your business will become in five years? What will you need to do for your business to reach these goals?

The Business Plan

Writing a business plan helps you focus on the future of your business. It helps you set goals. Start your plan with where your business is today. Include what you hope it to be like in three or five years.

A business plan describes your business. It states what you are selling. It tells *who* will use your product or service. It tells *why* someone will use your product or service. It lists the suppliers

27

Mark Blifield owns a coffee farm in Kona, Hawaii. Kona coffee is the only coffee grown in the United States. Mr. Blifield has chosen an extremely successful product to market.

of your product or service. It lists your major competitors.

Your business plan should include the name and address of your business. It should identify you as the owner.

A business plan also includes a financial report of the money invested in your business. It should list your income and your estimated expenses. The difference between the money you take in and the money you spend is the company's profit. If a business makes a profit, the business plan is helpful in borrowing money.

Study the sample business plan on page 31. Use it to make a plan for the career you are considering. A business plan may help you decide if the career has the potential of being successful. It also may help you decide to search for a different career.

Wynn

I always liked working with machinery. I enjoyed shop classes in high school. During my senior year I worked several evenings a week for a company that cleaned offices.

At first, I washed the insides of windows. But after several months, I ran a heavy-duty carpet cleaner. I enjoyed running the sweeper: It was a specific job to do, and because most machines are noisy, I was totally on my own while I ran it.

By the second semester I knew that I wanted to

Audley O'Brien owns this company, Brooklyn Welding, Inc. There are entrepreneurial opportunities in many areas, such as the trades.

Sample Business Plan

Name of company: Name of owner:
Address:
Telephone: Hours of service:

Service/products:
Fees/charges:
Potential customers:
How customers will be reached (advertising, etc.):

Major competitors and why your service/product can compete:

Estimated start-up costs:
Estimated income:
Estimated expenses:
Estimated profit:

Estimated income in three years:
How I will achieve that income (get new customers, more products/services, get more training, hire help, etc.):

open my own carpet-cleaning business. I took several business classes, and I began to do some market research. I compared the prices of five companies that offered cleaning services. I checked the cost of buying my own machine. I called the newspaper to learn the price of advertising. I made a business plan to estimate how much money I would need to start up.

I had saved nearly a thousand dollars from my part-time job by graduation. Because I did not want to borrow money, I started my business on a lower scale than I first considered.

I found that it was cheaper to advertise by using coupons in a flyer mailed to nearby households than to run newspaper ads. I put an ad in the telephone book. I set up an office in the basement of my parents' home and installed a business phone.

During my first months in business, I rented a carpet sweeper when a customer called with a job. Business was very slow, so I decided to market more aggressively. I had business cards printed and began mailing them to small businesses.

After six months, I had a second batch of flyers distributed. The weather began to get cool. I guess when people stay home more, they like to have their carpets cleaned. Or perhaps the second coupon mailing was more successful, but anyway business began to pick up.

Four months later my business began to break even. Three months after that, I bought a heavy-duty carpet sweeper.

My company is four years old now. I still run it out of my parents' basement, but I am looking for an inexpensive store to rent. I own several machines. When I get an office-cleaning contract, I hire students

Anyone can start their own business. Many kids take advantage of hot summer weather to set up lemonade stands.

to help me at night. I handle the day jobs myself.

After I find a store, I hope to expand my business. I plan to rent out my machines when I am not using them. I may sell cleaning supplies.

Owning my own business has been a lot of work, but it is fun. I would not want to spend my time any other way!

Questions to Ask Yourself

Prepare yourself before you start your business. It's important to have a very good idea what your business will do and what its profits will be before opening. Here are some questions to help you get ideas about getting your business off the ground. 1) What information would you include in your business plan? 2) What are some methods of advertising your service or business?

CHAPTER 3

MANAGING YOUR BUSINESS

Businesses are owned in one of four principal ways, which differ widely in style of operation.

Forms of Ownership

A business owned by only one person is called a sole proprietorship. The owner makes all decisions and takes total responsibility for the business. The sole owner also receives all the profits.

When more than one person owns a business it is called a partnership. Partners share income, expenses, work, and management of the business. Another form of partnership is a silent partner. In this form of ownership one owner often manages the company. The silent partner invests money and shares in the business's profit. A silent partner usually does not work in the company.

The corporation is a third form of business

ownership. Corporations are regulated by the state in which they operate. Corporations protect the owners from lawsuits. But corporations are expensive to set up and require advice from a lawyer. Some owners wait until a business shows a large profit before they incorporate.

A franchise is another way to start a business. Franchises are chains of businesses that operate under the same name but with separate owners. The head company receives an upfront fee and a percentage of the profit made by the individual businesses. The head company is similar to a silent partner who gets a share of the profit.

Franchise fees are expensive. The upfront fee often runs to $15,000 or more. In 1993 more than 4,000 franchise companies were operating in sixty industries.

Franchises offer an entrepreneur the opportunity to sell a well-known product. The entrepreneur also benefits from the head company's name, background, and experience.

An entrepreneur needs to investigate the head company very carefully before buying a franchise. Franchises are not always a guarantee of financial success. A buyer could lose a life's savings on a bad choice.

Legal Protection

You may want to protect your ideas and inventions with a patent or copyright. Literary work,

A partnership is one type of business ownership.

art work, software programs, and songs or films can be protected with a copyright. For specific information on copyright, write to the Library of Congress, Washington, DC 20339; telephone: 202-479-0700.

An invention or a new product can be protected with a patent from the Patent Office. For specific information about patents, write to The Superintendent of Documents, U.S. Government Printing Office, Washington, DC 20402; telephone: 202-557-7800.

Legal Obligations

Get a social security number and card if you do not already have one. The number of your local Social Security office is listed in your phone book. You will need a social security number for legal transactions such as bank accounts and tax payment credits.

Check with City Hall to find out what is required to start a business. You may need a business registration permit or a license.

Your city may have zoning laws regulating home businesses. Ask about that at City Hall if you are planning to work from your home. Often there are few requirements if you do not hire regular employees.

If you plan to hire employees, check on employment regulations. You must pay local, state, and federal taxes on an employee's wages. Your business also must pay social security tax, unemployment tax, disability tax, and workers' compensation tax for employees.

All businesses are required to file federal and state income tax returns every year. Even a sole proprietorship must pay a self-employment tax.

You may need liability insurance for your business. Liability insurance protects a business against customer suits. This insurance often is expensive. Talk with a lawyer to see if you need it. Check with City Hall or the Chamber of

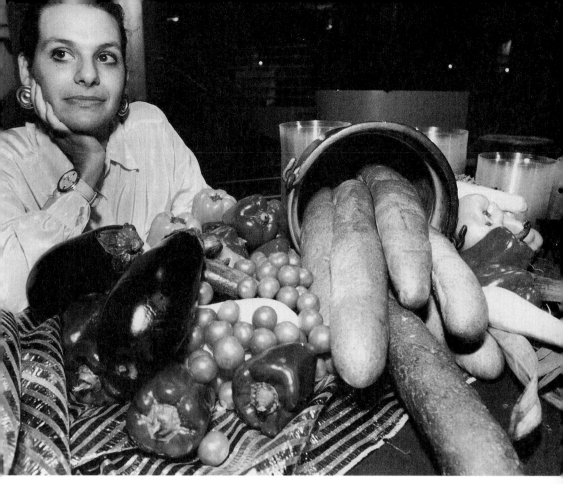

A key to having a successful business is to offer a unique service. Robyn Webb's catering company, "A Pinch of Thyme," offers only low-fat foods.

Commerce for information about these obligations. They can explain anything that you do not understand.

Recordkeeping

You must keep daily business records. An accountant who is skilled at dealing with business records can advise you on how to start your business and how to keep good records. An experienced accountant often saves money in the long run.

You must learn to keep accurate records including inventory, incoming cash, bills, and bank statements.

A business checking account can enable you to keep a record of your income deposits and expenses paid. File all bank statements, receipts, and bills. Business records must be kept as proof for tax purposes. You should keep all canceled checks, receipts, and a copy of your income tax forms for at least seven years.

Good recordkeeping also keeps you in control of your business, organizing the necessary paperwork.

Accounts Receivable is the money your customers owe your business. Obviously, it is best if your customers pay cash or as soon as possible. Accounts Payable is the money your business owes for expenses and supplies.

You can keep these records in a spiral notebook or a ledger. A ledger is a book of lined paper with vertical columns. Separate ledger pages should be kept for Accounts Receivable (income) and Accounts Payable (expenses) each month.

The ledger sheets on the next page are examples of good records.

Profit-and-Loss Statement

At the end of each month you will need to prepare a Profit-and-Loss Statement, or "P & L." This is a summary of the balance between your income and your expenses. That difference shows whether your business made or lost money. The

Sample Ledger Sheet for Accounts Receivable

NAME OF YOUR COMPANY
Accounts Receivable for Month of _____

Date	Name of Customer	Amount	Due
		$	.
			.
			.
			.
			.

Sample Ledger Sheet for Accounts Payable

NAME OF YOUR COMPANY
Accounts Payable for the Month of_____

Date	Expense	Check #	Amount
			$.
			.
			.
			.

P & L statement can help you see if you need to reduce your costs.

Remember, new businesses often show a loss for some time before they begin to show a profit.

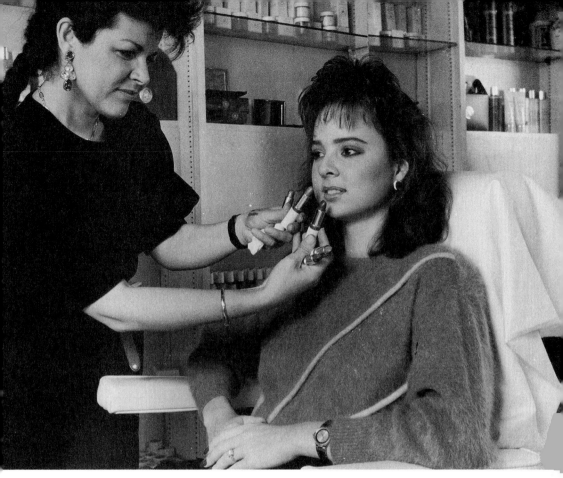

Sometimes a part-time job can help you get your own business started.

Do not become discouraged if you do not make a profit immediately.

The Profit-and-Loss statement on the next page shows the net amount of money a business made after expenses.

Eli

During high school I worked three nights a week and weekends at a yogurt store. Mr. Mitchell, the owner, was near retirement age. He treated me like a son and taught me to run the business. Besides serving

43

Sample Profit and Loss Statement

NAME OF YOUR COMPANY

DATE _____

Total (gross) Income	$ 500.00
Cost of Products Sold	−150.00
Gross (total) Profit	$ 350.00
Operating Expenses	
Supplies	$ 10.00
Advertising	225.00
Rent/telephone, etc.	30.00
Total Operating Expenses	$ 265.00
Total Income	$ 350.00
Total Operating Expenses	−265.00
Net Profit	$ 80.00

customers, *I helped prepare bank deposits and kept records.*

Last year Mr. Mitchell decided to retire. He offered me a "working partnership" to run the business for him. I would receive the same hourly salary, but each year 10 percent of the store's profit would be invested in my share of the business.

In five years, 50 percent of the store's profit will be

This man used his skills as a graphic artist to begin a free-lance business.
He works from his home.

invested in my partnership. I will have a "buy-out" option to buy Mr. Mitchell's shares, or I can remain a working partner and take 50 percent of the store's profit in cash.

I love the yogurt business. The hours are long, but I enjoy the work. I like dealing with the customers. Sometimes I get frustrated when the machines break down during our peak hours. I also do not like it when my part-time employees don't show up for work. But the challenges of this business are no more than those of other businesses.

I never dreamed that my part-time job would lead to such a rare business opportunity. I know that 70 percent of all partnerships break up within two years, but ours is different. I never could have found enough capital to start a business on my own. I am very lucky to benefit from Mr. Mitchell's brains and money in return for my time and effort.

Questions to Ask Yourself

You will need to decide many things before starting your own business. Make sure you know the answers to these questions. 1) What form of business most appeals to you: sole proprietorship, partnership, corporation, or franchise—and why? 2) What are the basic steps to managing a business? 3) How would you go about setting up a business?

Ben Cohen, right, and Jerry Greenfield, the famous Vermont ice cream makers, promote their new Ben and Jerry's Peace Pop.

Mary Kay Cosmetics, founded by entrepreneur Mary Kay Ash, is now a
multi-million dollar business.

CHAPTER 4

SUCCESS AS AN ENTREPRENEUR

The number of new small businesses has increased steadily during the past thirty years. In 1991, about 20.5 million business tax returns were filed. Most of these businesses were small and medium-sized companies. Fewer than 7,000 of them were large enough to employ 500 employees.

The American economy is changing. The workplace is always changing. That means you may have several different careers during your lifetime. Remember that when you choose a career.

A successful career takes planning and preparation. Business courses can help you run your business. Technical, vocational training, or college courses can help prepare you for your business.

Entrepreneurs need experience and education. They must believe in their ability to succeed. **49**

Tomima Edmark's invention, Topsy Tail, was inspired
by her love of knitting.

They must be willing to take chances. They must
be able and willing to work hard. They must
research the marketplace to understand the competition. They must be able to adapt to changing
circumstances.

Jade

*My hobby has been making puppets since I was
about ten years old. I have more than fifty puppets
in my collection.*

During middle school and high school I gave

puppet shows for children's birthday parties. I charged

An entrepreneur can begin a business as big as McDonald's or as small as a streetside fruit stand.

ten dollars for a half-hour party show. During the summers I gave puppet shows for young children in the neighborhood. I charged a quarter admission for a half-hour show.

By the end of eleventh grade I was considering turning my hobby into a career. I made three sample animal puppets, keeping a record of how much time each one took to make and the cost of supplies.

The sample puppets were cute and had a lot of child-appeal. But two things kept me from marketing them. First, I wanted to keep them for my collection; I just did not want to sell something I had created. Second, the responsibility of running my own business seemed overwhelming.

The more I thought about what I wanted to do after high school, the more undecided I became. I did not want to go to college right away, but I did not want to look for a job either.

During my senior year I took three courses to prepare me to become an entrepreneur: personal computers, recordkeeping, and business.

In business class I learned that in 1992 there were 5.5 million salespeople in the direct-sales industry. Almost 60% of the $14.1 billion made in retail sales during 1992 was made from one-on-one sales between a customer and the salesperson. Only about 20% of that total was made though group sales or party plan selling.

Even so, I found the idea of party plan selling very appealing. I knew that I wanted to become an

Richard E. LaMotta invented the phenomenally successful Chipwich—ice cream sandwiched between two chocolate chip cookies.

independent sales contractor. Giving in-home party demonstrations was similar to giving puppet shows. I found that exciting.

I researched some of the direct sales companies: Discovery Toys, NSA, BeautiControl, Network 2000, Pampered Chef, Multiples at Home, Park Lane International, and Tupperware.

I became an independent contractor for Tupperware three years ago. The Tupperware company trained me to give home demonstrations. We have a support network with weekly meetings where we discuss marketing. The meetings are great in keeping me motivated.

When I first started as a consultant I made about $500 a month. Now I am an executive manager, and I earn around $20,000 a year. I give most of my party demonstrations in the evenings, so I actually work part time.

During the day I take several business courses at junior college. My classes build on the practical experience I get from my business.

If you want to *make* a job, not just *take* a job, a career inside the world of entrepreneurs may be for you. Your future is in your own hands. Plan for it. Prepare for it. Look forward to it. And enjoy it!

Questions to Ask Yourself

Preparation is the key to having a successful business. If you know what you want to do and how

You can learn a trade such as carpentry and begin your own business.
Your career is in your own hands.

to do it well, you have a good chance of succeeding! 1) What kinds of activities can you do now to help prepare yourself for a career as an entrepreneur? 2) What skills, interests, or talents do you possess now that might later help you run your own business?

ORGANIZATIONS TO CONTACT

The U.S. Small Business Administration (SBA) offers programs and services to help entrepreneurs. These include training, educational programs, publications, and advice.

The SBA has offices around the country. Look in your telephone directory under "U.S. Government" to find the office nearest you. You may also call: 1-800-8-ASK-SBA; FAX: 202-205-7064.

The National Association for the Self-Employed (NASE) offers information and services to members. NASE was founded in 1981 by a group of self-employed business owners. NASE offers a toll-free hot line, business consultants, health care programs, and travel discounts. Call: 1-800-232-NASE.

The Service Corps of Retired Executives Association (SCORE) provides information, business help, training, and workshops for entrepreneurs.

SCORE has more than 380 chapters around

the country. Its counselors have helped over 2.5 million clients since 1964. A SCORE counselor can review your business plan before you take it to your banker. For further information, call: 1-800-634-0245; or write: SCORE, 409 Third Street SW, Washington, DC 20024.

Many colleges and junior colleges have Small Business Development Centers or Career Centers. You need not be a student at the college to get free information and advice.

Colleges and junior colleges often offer noncredit workshops that are helpful to entrepreneurs. Workshops are a good way to upgrade your skills.

Look under "Schools" in the yellow pages of your phone directory for names and phone numbers.

In Canada, contact the Canadian Federation of Independent Business at #401, 4141 Yonge Street, Willowdale, ON M2P 2A6. Their phone number is (401) 222-8022. You can also contact the Canadian Organization of Small Business, Inc. at Box 11246, M.P.O., Edmonton, AB T5H 3J5. Their phone number is (403) 423-2672.

GLOSSARY

accountant Person who examines and keeps business accounts.

accounts payable Money or accounts that a business owes.

accounts receivable Money or accounts owed to a business.

business plan Outline of products or services, resources and money needed, goals, and a plan to reach those goals.

competition Other companies that try to get customers for similar businesses.

credit Obtaining products or services by agreeing to pay for them later.

entrepreneur Person who owns his or her own business.

franchise Agreement between two companies to allow an independently owned company to use the parent company's name, product, trademark, and operating methods.

gross profit Total income before expenses.

ledger Book of ruled paper with columns to help keep records.

marketing Finding a buyer for a product.

net profit Income after deducting expenses.

partnership Business owned by two or more persons who share income, expenses, and work.

Profit-and-Loss Statement Summary of the balance between a company's income and expenses.

quality control Methods used to make sure a product is always of the same quality.

sole proprietorship Company owned by one person.

FOR FURTHER READING

Ashworth, Tanya. *Caring for Kids*. Denver: Vade Mecum Press, 1989.

Barrett, Linda, and Guengerich, Galen. *Personal Services*. New York: Franklin Watts, 1991.

Berman, Steve, and Weiss, Vivian. *What to Be*. Englewood Cliffs, NJ: Prentice-Hall, 1980.

Dunnan, Nancy. *Entrepreneurship*. Englewood Cliffs: Silver Burdette Press, 1990.

Goldstein, Arnold S., PhD. *Starting on a Shoestring*. New York: John Wiley & Sons, 1991.

Maul, Lyle R., MBA, and Mayfield, Dianne Craig, JD. *The Entrepreneur's Road Map*. Alexandria: Saxtons River Pub., 1990.

Mitchell, Joyce Slayton. *Jobs and Career Planning*. New York: College Board Publications, 1990.

Paradis, Adrian A. *Opportunities in Vocational and Technical Careers*. Chicago: National Textbook Co., 1992.

————. *Planning Your Career of Tomorrow.* Chicago: National Textbook Co., 1986.

Schniderman, Jeffery R. and Hurwitz, Sue. *Applications: A Guide to Filling Out All Kinds of Forms.* New York: Rosen Publishing Group, 1994.

Thomas, Martha. *Guide to Outdoor Careers.* Harrisburg, PA: Stackpole Books, 1981.

Wittenberg, Renee. *Opportunities in Child Care Careers.* Chicago: National Textbook Co., 1987.

INDEX

ABOUT THE AUTHOR
Sue Hurwitz holds an MA in Education from the University of Missouri. She has taught every grade, K–9. Sue is the coauthor of *Drugs and Your Friends, Hallucinogens, Drugs and Birth Defects,* and *Applications: A Guide to Filling Out All Kinds of Forms.*

COVER PHOTO: © David Maung/Impact Visuals
PHOTO CREDITS: p. 24 © Dan Habib/Impact Visuals; p. 26 © Peter Miller/The Image Bank; p. 33 © Don Klumpp/Image Bank; p. 45 © Robert Phillips/The Image Bank; p. 55 © L.L.T. Rhodes/The Image Bank; all other photos © AP/Wide World Photos
PHOTO RESEARCH: Vera Ahmadzadeh with Jennifer Croft
DESIGN: Kim Sonsky